MW00823672

BOOM
AND THEN IT CAME

ELLEN AREVALO-BARRERA

©2020 Ellen Arevalo-Barrera. All rights reserved. No part of this publication may be reproduced, distributed, or transmitted in any form or by any means, including photocopying, recording, or other electronic or mechanical methods, without the prior written permission of the author, except in the case of brief quotations embodied in critical reviews and certain other noncommercial uses permitted by copyright law.
ISBN: 978-1-09833-127-6

*W*HEN I THINK OF MY CHILDHOOD, I THINK I DIDN'T have it all that bad. I dealt with my parents' separation at fourteen but managed my emotions in my own way. Mom (aka Grandma Rosey) and Dad (aka Pal) had a very argumentative marriage; Mom sobbed a lot, and Dad wrapped himself up at work. I was forced to grow up quickly, help Mom emotionally to get through it all. I think I did the best I could. I had a blessed life, was a healthy kid, finished high school, and went on to college. I began my career and married my high school sweetheart. Fast forward: We have a beautiful daughter together, Elle. Elle (aka Boom) was born healthy but she had a hard time coming out into this world. I was induced because I was overdue. Now, I know what her hesitation was. It's like she knew it all along… Boom was going to face a very challenging time, and this was nothing compared to what I have been through. My parents' marriage falling apart was certainly peanuts compared to what she was about to embrace during her teen years.

Boom was born on a cold winter day. As she was growing up, always had this sense of maturity, and I guess it's because she was surrounded more by adults than children. She was a quiet kid and was kept busy with sports, theatre, music, and school. I figured she needed to keep busy; she had no siblings, and I didn't want her to get bored. She loves school and takes after me as I always enjoyed doing school work (I was known as a teacher's pet).

We always try to find our definition of life. Sometimes people live a very long life and they never find it. Coincidentally, Boom had asked me at some point in her mist of puberty why she was put on this earth. Gosh, how I thought to myself how did we (my hubby and I) create a child so inquisitive and so deep in thoughts. At that age, I wasn't asking my mom and dad those questions.

Boom was finishing up seventh grade. I remember it like it was yesterday—such a vivid memory. It was early May 2019. She started complaining about body aches and pains. At first, we thought it's just due to sports or her menstrual cycle. She was showering one day, and she looked very pale. She said she felt like she was going to pass out. I put her in bed; it was a school day and she told me, "Mom, I'll be fine, let me just rest a little and I will be ready to take the finals." I was nervous and I called out from work because she just didn't look well. She insisted I drive her to finish her finals. So I did, but I sat in the school parking lot and together, we left the minute she was done. Summer school break started. It was time for her yearly physical exam anyway, so we took her to the doctor. Of course, routine blood work was done. We told a doctor that she's been having constant pain in her body and also that she didn't want to laugh because her chest hurt simply by giggling. We were told it was "growing pains." Boy! Do I cringe when I think about it today! Blood results were normal; she was just encouraged to take multivitamins for her anemia. Nothing alarming, so we went on living, so to speak.

June arrived, school was out, and Boom tagged along on a business trip with me to Florida, she was my roommate for the next couple of nights. The first night, I didn't get much sleep as she was moaning in pain during her sleep. I nudged her a few times and asked if she was alright. She said she was fine and responded, "Mom, this happens every night; you don't hear me because I'm in my own room." The next few nights left me a bit concerned as my little girl was in pain at nights. We flew back home and I told my husband we would need to take her back to the doctor because what I witnessed wasn't "growing pains." My husband took her to a different doc immediately, and this time we were told to do more blood work. Blood work was going to take a day or so for the results. The next day, I was headed to work, and my husband calls me to tell me he had received a call from the doc to admit her to the hospital as soon as possible for more testing. I caught an Uber back home to meet them. This is where my life was about to have a new meaning, and she was going to find out exactly what her mission was. I kept a journal throughout our journey and wanted to share my experience as a parent and caretaker of a hero.

June 25, 2019

I checked-in to the local hospital with Boom and my hubby for further testing. We packed up for the night since we already knew that she had to be monitored and we were to await blood results. A doc in hospital told us directly that it may be a virus she's fighting, or it could be "cancer." He said that flat out to all three of us including my daughter in the room. Boom immediately said, "Am I going to lose my hair?" As a parent, I was in pure shock and desperately wanted to scream and cry out loud. But I didn't want to accept it because it could be the worst case scenario. I stepped out of the room with the doctor and asked her if it was protocol to be that direct, considering she was breaking the news to a teenage kid. She confirmed that it was their way of doing things. I shared that as a parent, I would've expected to hear the news first then deliver the news to my child. But no going back now, what's done is done. Tomorrow, we will await the true results.

June 26, 2019

Long night yesterday—tossed and turned—couldn't sleep in that cot. All I did was stare at her and kept thinking how we got there. Did I fail as a parent and didn't nourish her enough? I prayed so hard that this would all just go away. Or that I was caught in a nightmare and someone at some point would wake me up, and things would be back to normal. They gave her two rounds of blood transfusion this morning. Around noon, a nurse came in and re-assigned us to a bigger room. I guess by that time the team knew the results. At about 2:00 p.m., the same doctor from yesterday came in, and I was in positive spirits and believed she would just tell us it's a virus. Unfortunately, she told me to sit down. I knew then it wasn't going to be good news. She told us it was leukemia (ALL) and explained the whole diagnosis. Her words sounded so far away, like I was stuck in a tunnel, and I could faintly here her words.. I held Boom tight as she sobbed on the bed. I kept on saying, "It's going to be okay; we will get through this." She just kept on thinking about losing her hair. I held my baby in my arms and was completely devastated. My hubby looked towards the window and continued to ask questions about treatment and asked if they were one hundred percent sure, as tears fell down his cheek. My mom, Grandma Rosey, was in the room too and she yelled, crying hysterically. I kept on thinking what we did so wrong in life that would hurt my child like this. Tomorrow she's scheduled for a bone marrow biopsy. God give me the strength to be strong for her.

June 27, 2019

Boom is in pain after her biopsy. They said it was normal and gave her some pain medications. She's still getting hydrated. The doc wants to start chemo treatment tomorrow; however, we are looking to move to a new hospital that is very well known for treating cancer. We are calling a few hospitals today and checking with the insurance company.

June 28, 2019

We did check out in the afternoon and were able to see a new doctor at the new hospital. Everything flowed well yesterday. We were discharged and were able to drive on our own and met the new team of doctors. They explained the whole treatment process. It became more real today as we saw many kids and families in the hallways sharing the same journey. We were scheduled to come in this morning; however, Boom had so much pain in her right leg that we needed to rush in the middle of the night and bring her to the hospital. They gave her heavy painkiller meds to calm her down. X-rays were done. We met with surgeon to discuss mediport placement. Boom will now get a line on her chest to receive chemo. She started her first round of chemo.

She immediately felt nauseous. Long day... things happened too quickly. I guess that was a good thing, it would heal her faster. She's resting now.

June 30, 2019

Uncle Phil from North Carolina came to visit us... what a nice surprise. She played games, especially Connect 4, with both uncles. Uncle Pete came to visit too. We meet in the family room at the hospital and spent time together. All that's going through my mind is how we got here. I know that in this hospital, she will receive the best care. We know many family and friends that were treated here and are survivors today. I wish I could fast forward time.

July 3, 2019

It's been a crazy few days at the hospital. My focus has been on learning new medications. She also had her mediport placed on her chest. This was tough. I dressed up in a surgeon's gear, and we wheeled her all the way down these long hallways to the surgery room. Never imagined to walk these cold hallways. I held her hand and did the sign of the cross and trusted God would help her through this. She's nauseous and feels yucky. We are finally back home, and she will be an outpatient for most of her treatments. So far, there was no hair loss. Boom is having a hard time swallowing pills. I was given a pill crusher to put into her applesauce but it's so chalky and disgusting. We also try a syringe for liquid meds so she can swallow it quickly, but all she does is gag. I try to taste all the meds she's having so I can describe them to her. My kid has never even taken a Tylenol for her cramps and now she needs to take a handful of medications. The team here helps her to learn how to swallow pills. They try with candy first. I personally don't like pills. I hate it more seeing my kid take these things. They also stopped her period by giving her birth control as part of the treatment.

July 4, 2019

Happy Birthday America! We had Boom's music teacher come over since she doesn't feel that well to go out. She finds joy in singing and playing her ukulele. I also feel it distracts her for a bit and allows her to still enjoy her hobbies. It's got to be a struggle, feeling like this and still having interests in things—in life, in general. I encourage her to stay strong and kick ass.

July 5, 2019

We went back to the hospital today for a spinal tap and chemo treatment. She feels beat up and is not in the mood to eat much. I bring her snacks from home just in case she craves something. She's beginning to feel tired. She's beginning to lose weight. I see my little girl transforming—physically and emotionally. They have good resources here; we have a meditator that comes by and puts her in a positive state of mind. There are also team members that check up on the kids and play card games or do anything they want. Boom is getting to be good at UNO. I even have her doing word searches with me since I love word puzzles.

July 8, 2019

Boom wasn't feeling well. She passed out in shower. Luckily, she didn't hurt her head. I was there with her. So, I screamed to call my hubby to help me. He got her out of the bathroom. I called our doc and he told me to call 911 and have an ambulance bring her to the hospital. EMS came—her sugar was over 500. It was scary to see her out of it. EMS was so kind to take us to our hospital directly. The usual protocol is to take you to a local hospital. However, the EMS worker was on the phone with our doc and confirmed that they would wait for us. I rode in the ambulance with her, and sirens were going off as we made it into busy New York City. It was an awful ride. My first time; it sure was bumpy. Similar to what our days are going to look like. We are here for a few days.

July 9, 2019

Her sugar is still high, they are starting to give her insulin ... We've seen her body go through so many ups and downs; low heart rate, high heart rate. It's all these medicines doing their jobs in her body. These treatments really knock her out. She sleeps a lot.

July 11, 2019

The nurses started training me to do insulin shots on her so when we get out of here, I could start doing it at home. As long as she's on these steroids, her sugar won't be back to normal. We never had any sugar problems. But steroids are part of this chemo-induction period. We had visitors today, my hubby's co-workers are super sweet and they came to visit Boom. A few of them are also cancer survivors so they definitely are a great resource for Boom. She can meet other strong ladies that have fought this terrible disease.

July 12, 2019

It is yet another round of spinal tap today. These treatments include giving her chemo into her spinal cord. Seeing my little girl's eyes roll back as they inject anesthesia into her in a cold procedure room was terrifying. The medical team is comforting and reassures us that Boom will be fine. I held her hand and said a little prayer as they counted backwards. After the treatment, we had the hospital music therapist visit us. Again, music gives Boom comfort. I went to the chapel downstairs and prayed for her. I hate leaving her side even if it is for a few minutes. I helped her to the bathroom and held her head as she puked her guts out. I also put a cold towel on her head to ease her a bit.

July 17, 2019

Boom has her highs and lows. Her music teacher came to visit her at the hospital. The tunes put her at ease for about an hour. She also got a massage by the famous masseuse here. She loves doing slime; it soothes her. My hubby and I also attended a yoga parents' session to ease us a bit. We have a hospital roomie—a little girl battling cancer. Sucks! Cancer hits any age.

July 19, 2020

Boom had a spinal tap today. Her hair is starting to fall; it's on the pillow covers. I clean it while she's not looking. The bed is so uncomfortable for her. We miss being home. I did a bit of laundry today. I washed her blanket that she loves so much; she's had that blanket since she was a baby.

July 20, 2019

The inhouse music teacher at the hospital gave her a new guitar to play around with. Grandma Rosey came to visit and brought us some home-cooked food. I went to the church across the street and prayed. I always had faith, but this experience has certainly increased my faith. I think whatever faith you believe in, you should hold on tight to it. Faith and hope help you in desperate times.

July 23, 2019

We got discharged today after almost three weeks. It's wonderful being home. I cooked and was able to have some homemade food. We missed our comfy beds. We got into our pajamas after a long warm shower. It's so calming—not having to listen to the constant beep of machines, or nurses constantly waking you up for meds or vitals. We are going to get a good night's sleep tonight (sipping on merlot as I write this).

July 24, 2019

Boom put on makeup today to cover her pale skin. She feels yucky and looks herself in the mirror and is not happy with what she is seeing. I tell her she's a beauty, that her skin will glow soon after this treatment is finished. She's starting to see more of her dead hair come off. I hold as strong as I can in these moments.

July 28, 2019

We had family over and it was nice being together after a long time being in the hospital. Grandma Rosey came to cook and made Boom her favorite dishes. Her taste buds continue to disappear. She says certain foods are not the same. I celebrate when she takes a few bites from her meals. We are having a quiet summer through this all. Everyone around us is enjoying the summer break and here we are spending our time in and out of the hospital. I know this time next year; we will be in a different place.

July 30, 2019

Boom went in for a platelet transfusion. She had an appetite when we came out. She was in the mood for chicken fajitas at our local Mexican restaurant. I was so down to have me a margarita! She's such a trooper. Boom's hair is falling out more. I comb her hair on the outside deck so she doesn't see it on the floor inside our home. I take a grocery bag and place the dead hair in the bag. I had alopecia about two years ago so I guess it prepared me to see hair loss. But for it to be my baby losing hair, it's so sad.

July 31, 2019

She was in the mood to go shopping, so we went to Target and picked up a few things. She's added orange into her wardrobe these days because orange is the pediatric cancer color. She's grateful for those cake pops and cold raspberry iced teas at Starbucks. She also had physical therapy today. We have a nurse that comes over to our home and helps with her walking. With bi-weekly spinal taps, she limps while walking. We meditate a lot these days; it helps her sleep. After being on steroids so long, she has insomnia and doesn't sleep well at night. But at least her sugar is back to a normal level.

August 2, 2019

We met with the doctor today to brainstorm about new treatments as this chemo is not too effective. We are looking to do a stem cell treatment. It is unbelievable how science is. So, we are extracting her t-cells, collecting them, and then sending them off to a lab. The science laboratory works with her cells to clean them up, then they put it back into her body and are programmed to kill the cancer cells in her body. It's fascinating, but I feel like my kid is a science project. Actually, those are Boom's exact words. I say we try things that are going to work. I was pretty direct with the doctors on this. I came to this specific hospital to see positive results. I had a complete breakdown today and had to excuse myself out of the office and ran to the bathroom to cry.

August 5, 2019

We walked on the beach, heard the waves, and breathed in the fresh air. Boom decided to shave off her head. Our favorite hairdresser came over and did it for her. It was a tough day, since she had such thick, beautiful hair. Boom is such a brave young girl. I explained that her hair will eventually grow back, even better than before. My heart just melts. After so many days in the hospital, it's so nice to be home. I don't think I ever appreciated my home so much until now.

August 7, 2019

Boom had a second temporary line put in her chest today to do the t-cell extraction this week. I hate walking that hallway into that cold procedure room. My heart just comes out of my chest. I feel so ill and scared. I held her hand until they did another round of anesthesia. What I would give to switch roles. I want to take all the pain from her.

August 8, 2019

Today the stem cell collection took place. It took about six hours. She didn't feel too well. We stopped a couple of times because she was feeling like she was going to pass out. They kept on giving her tums and orange juice. It was quite interesting though. It was this huge machine which was collecting her t-cells. Her body is bloated, especially her face. She's tired but enjoys playing UNO still. Boom has moved up to UNO emoji.

August 9, 2019

The temporary second line on her chest was removed today. It was nice to see a rainbow in the sky as we drove home after treatment. It showed us that there is hope in all this and this too shall pass. She will have all these scars on her chest once this mission is complete. Boom will always see these wounds, and I hope it will keep her grounded.

August 10, 2019

I bought a wig at a local wig store today and she's killing it with it! My friend's daughter came over and did Boom's makeup and nails. She felt more like a teen today. She's so beautiful and it's a shame she doesn't even see it. As a normal teen, you go through confidence issues but this experience just puts it to a different level. I can only stay positive and continue to be her cheerleader.

August 15, 2019

Boom had another spinal tap today. We have more transfusions today, both blood and platelets. My coworker came to visit us. He told me the office gossip. I don't miss work at all as what matters is that I'm with Boom every step of the way. How life changes. Unfortunately, I've always been guilty of putting work before family. Sometimes you go through tough battles so that you may learn lessons. Believe me, I've learned a lot of life lessons through all this.

August 16, 2019

We went to the beach today and had a picnic. Took a blanket, sandwiches, and drinks and sat on the sand. We played a little music and appreciated the water and beautiful sky. We count our blessings that it's about two months in and she's kicking ass. I'm glad Boom has been able to have both of us—my hubby and I—every step of the way. We are both on leave from work and haven't left her side. We are going into our 20th wedding anniversary next year and this chapter of our lives is only making us stronger as a couple and as a family. We are so grateful for hubby's job that offers great health benefits. Medical bills can be another layer of worry when still paying for mortgage and other financial responsibilities.

August 22, 2019

Boom had more chemo today. It's crazy how chemo wasn't the right treatment for her but we still need to do another round because not doing anything will increase her leukemia cells. She was back to feeling nauseous again. This week will probably take another toll on her body. School is back in session soon next month, so Boom is starting to feel anxious on whether she will be okay to go back and what her class-mates will think. I told her that it will be fine. "Don't focus on what others are going to think, just focus on you getting better!"

August 25, 2019

We had a family barbecue; it was a beautiful day. Boom wasn't much in the mood to come out in the yard but she was a trooper with the family over and still managed to have a smile on her face. My aunt from Florida came to visit us. It was nice to have family around; we are lucky to have them and their endless prayers. Boom feels the love and is thankful of the support system we have.

August 26, 2019

We had spinal tap today. These days are tough as she gets both spinal tap and chemo. She continues to have some restless nights. She uses the Calm app and ASMR- Audio Sensory Meridian Response on Youtube- to help her sleep. She loves her Beats headphones that give her that privacy. I check up on her in the middle of the night when I get up for my bathroom breaks. I pray she has sweet dreams tonight and gets rest.

September 1, 2019

We had family over. Boom is so fortunate and blessed we have Grandmas, a Great-Grandma, Aunts and Uncles that shower her with love. Family is important during these times. It takes a village to get through battles. There are people out there that don't have family and are alone and afraid. I pray that they find some comfort.

September 4, 2019

It's my birthday today. My birthday wish is for Boom to kick cancer's ass, and I know she will. I literally gave birth to my hero. Tomorrow is the first day of school. She's so excited! We've shopped for everything under the sun. It's a half-day tomor- row, so we will start her off slow. I'm a little hesitant in leaving Boom there the whole school day. I told her she knows her body and will know when it's time for a time out.

September 5, 2019

First day of eighth grade! She's all dressed up in her uniform. Boom put on her wig and make-up. So proud of her for getting up and looking forward to her last school year in the same school she's been since Pre-Kindergarten. Thank God for her teach- ers and principal who have been so supportive. I'm super proud of her for having the energy to get up early and look forward to a new day.

September 12, 2019

Boom was in the mood for pupusas. We took a ride out with Grandma Rosey to New Jersey and ate well. I'm so happy when she craves things, and I'm happy to fulfill her food cravings. It's not often she eats, so I try my very best to give her food she enjoys. Sometimes it's instant, so I have to run and get it for her! She craves various drinks and snacks like Snapple & Arizona iced tea, animal crackers, powdered white doughnuts, chocolate munchkins, surprisingly the eucharist (bread) from church—however couldn't get that. Believe me I asked our priest but it can't leave the House of God.

September 16, 2019

We went out for ice cream with Boom's friend and she also got her manicure and pedicure done. It is so nice to have people around to help us. The nail lady at the salon I go to—she's so sweet and comes to our home. Boom's Godmother aka Nina keeps on sending Amazon gifts. Not a day goes by that she doesn't receive a shipment from her. I met Nina back in college when we began our career answering phones at a hotel. Again, we are so blessed to have family and friends that are with us in this crazy journey.

September 19, 2019

Boom wanted to do some window shopping, so we went to check out the new outlets by the Staten Island Ferry. We walked around with Grandma Rosey and had Boom's favorite Starbucks treats. The weather was beautiful and that place has amazing views of NYC—love how the Freedom Tower stands out.

September 21, 2019

The masseuse that I know and who has done at home massages for me before has agreed to do a house call for Boom. She is in such need for a relaxing massage. The massages below the head are a bit uncomfortable since she has mediport on her chest, the pressure bothers her. The mediport will not be removed until maybe a year from now until all treatment is done, and we are on the road to recovery.

September 26, 2019

One of my dearest friends from Georgia is in town and visited us at home. Boom is craving chicken fajitas again, so we went to our favorite Mexican local restaurant.

Their food is delicious and they always end up giving Boom's favorite dish on the house. She loves the fresh lemonade too, and I love my Cadillac margaritas.

September 27, 2019

Boom wants to feel better about her image so she asks me if she can get fake eyelashes. I book an appointment with a referral, and we went to someone locally and had it done. Boom loves them. She says she feels prettier. She's having a hard time with her physical appearance. She's gorgeous but again doesn't accept it.

September 28, 2019

Today was her TACHS – Test for Admission into Catholic High Schools -test. I asked if she can be separated from students in the room since again, we need to be mindful of germs. Boom said she felt good about the test. We went out for steak after. We go to our local steakhouse to get a nice piece of meat and all the salad you can eat. I love when she's in the mood to dress up and go out. Before her diagnosis, we were always out and about. So being indoors is a challenge but I know there are better days ahead.

September 30, 2019

Boom is doing well in school. The days we have appointments, she does school work remotely. All students have an iPad, so it's easy for her. Today was also graduation picture day! She looked amazing, and I am super proud of her. I always tell my hubby, "How did we make such a smart and brave kid?" Despite what her body is going through physically and emotionally, she still smiles like she's living the best life. God, please keep her safe.

October 4, 2019

We had to do an echo today to make sure her heart is okay before transplant. We are scheduled for all these preliminary exams before transplant in the next couple of weeks. We are excited and nervous to hear of a donor soon that will make her all better.

October 7, 2019

I went on a field trip with Boom and her class. Well, it was not much of a field trip; we attended a wake at church for someone very dear to the school community and had a chance to pray extra while I sat in church. She came home tired after a long day at school. She drinks a lot of water as it keeps her hydrated. We are starting to see some hair growth, light peach fuzz. She's lost a lot of weight—almost 45 lbs since June. She calls her bald head an "egg." Boom is so funny. She makes fun of herself. Her humor is still there.

October 11, 2019

I tagged along on another class trip with Boom. We visited one of the high schools she would like to attend. We already submitted our High School options after the exam day. She fell today, coming off the school bus. She scraped her knee and tore her uniform pants. She got up like Gumby and shook it off like nothing happened. I got band-aid from the nurse, and she was fine. The old Elle would be crying but now nothing really hurts her after now going into her fourth month of treatment. She wanted to get a pedicure too, so I took her and we went to buy new school pants.

October 14, 2019

We checked into the hospital for a couple of nights to prepare her for immuno-therapy and monitor her. We have a roommate again. It is bizarre how a lot of parents share this journey, but you never know until you too are living through it.

October 15, 2019

Uncle Pete came to see us today and spent time with us in the hospital room. He didn't stay too long since we have a roommate and we are mindful to not be that annoying roommate. We usually have a family room we can hang out on the same floor. Depending on how Boom feels, we go there. But today was a bed day for her. So, we played cards with Uncle Pete and talked.

October 17, 2019

Boom is ready to start her immunotherapy where she needs to carry a backpack for the next five weeks. She now has to lug around an extra book bag when she goes to school and bathroom (everywhere!). The treatment is constantly hooked up to her mediport. We have to come here every seven days to change the treatment bag so she doesn't run out of it. So, the countdown begins, we are being discharged today.

October 19, 2019

I took Boom to her therapy session. She sees a therapist weekly to help her with her emotions and have an added resource to help her through all these life changes. I appreciate that she tells me things. Sometimes it's tough for me to hear, but I love her honesty. I'm glad she came to us needing someone else to talk to besides me and my hubby. Boom really connects with the therapist, and I'm happy we found her. Boom also had a Halloween party at her friend's house. We dropped her off, and hubby & I enjoyed a happy hour. Boom's costume this year was a boxer. It definitely fits who she is—a champ. She's dressed in a costume and underneath all that, she's battling her cancer with a machine hooked up to her. But no one can really tell. We did a good job to camouflage it.

October 21, 2019

We went to the hospital to get her bag of immunotherapy changed. It was a quick visit; they drew her blood to check on her counts. So far so good. She actually feels better on this treatment than chemo. She wakes up nauseous. Sometimes she asks for the meds to help her with it, but more often she just manages it. She says, the less meds she takes, the better. She hates taking meds unless it's necessary.

October 26, 2019

It's been a few days I haven't written, but Boom continued the Halloween festivities and attended her Halloween party at school. She won the best costume. Hubby and I also attended the party with her. She had a great time. She laughed and danced with her classmates. I was so grateful that she's feeling better with immunotherapy treatment. She's more energetic, and we are starting to see some light at the end of the tunnel. It was a fun night, and we were all tired.

October 28, 2019

We went to the hospital again to get her bag of immunotherapy changed and took blood test. Blood counts are trending up so it's great to see that. Walking down these hallways, seeing so many families going through this, I pause. And after four months, I still don't know how we got here.

October 29, 2019

I attended mass with Boom. She was assigned to read one of the liturgies. As I sat back in those pews, I truly was grateful for what this journey has brought us. It has certainly put life into perspective. I went back to work recently, and I'm really considering resigning so I can focus on her recovery. Next month, she will need a transplant and we are going to go through some tougher times. I prayed for everything to work itself out.

October 31, 2019

Happy Halloween! Boom showed off her costume again. We picked her up from school and headed to Applebee's for an early dinner with Grandma Rosey. It's a beautiful weather day, and I can't wait for time to pass by quick and have her at that finish line when treatments are complete.

November 2, 2019

It's Boom's Confirmation and she looks beautiful. Her homeroom teacher this year is her sponsor. I appreciate everyone who has been there for her and our family. Boom is so special; she received a special blessing from Cardinal Timothy Dolan today. I know God will continue to hold her hand and help her through this. We had a nice intimate lunch after the ceremony. My friend, who's a photographer, did a photo shoot, and I'm glad he was able to capture these unforgettable moments. We have a possible bone marrow donor and should be able to start the process by the end of the month only if she's in remission. I can feel it. I know she will be—in God I trust. Remission has been hard to get to. We took a test last month and she still had about 20% cancer cells in her body. The goal is to be at 0% before we could go on to transplant. If we are not there yet, we still need to continue chemo.

November 6, 2019

We went to celebrate my hubby's birthday at our favorite steakhouse today. We went to change her immuno bag yesterday. She still feels good. She says she feels more energized with this treatment. She's still plugging away at school and focused.

November 9, 2019

Her backpack started beeping in the middle of the night. It was nothing I could fix. It wasn't the battery, so we had to go to the hospital to get it fixed. Of course, we are about two days away in getting that thing off of her.

November 11, 2019

Boom met with Make-A-Wish reps to discuss her wish. She wants to meet Billie Eillish. She loves her music and her unique style. Finally, the backpack immunotherapy ended! We went to hospital to unplug her. Now she's walking around without her buddy for a couple of weeks until we check into the hospital. She feels liberated, she says. We hope for some good news soon.

November 12, 2019

She had her pulmonary and dentist follow up today, so we could take care of the pre-transplant testing too. Everything went well. We are getting a bit nervous since transplant is around the corner.

November 14, 2019

Boom had a scheduled bone marrow test; we hope to be on remission! I'm praying hard. Almost five months into treatment, I just hope her body has responded to all these treatments. Amen! God give us some good news please.

November 15, 2019

Wonderful news! Our doc called and said Boom is in remission! I was so glad I baked these orange cupcakes to celebrate. I also bought Peppa Pig balloons; she loves Peppa! Now, we wait for an admission date to start the pre-treatment before transplant. Unfortunately, she has to go through chemo again; in addition, she has to receive radiation prior to transplant. It took a toll on her these past five months and she's now feeling better, her counts are back up. Now her body has to get beaten down again. God help us—help my baby, my only child.

November 16, 2019

Uncle Pete came over and we went out for dinner with Pal. We had a nice time and enjoyed being out, certainly taking advantage of it since we will be checking in soon and will be isolated for some time. We won't be able to go out to crowded areas; we need to be in complete gear as she's traveling to places in a mask and gloves.

November 19, 2019

We met with the doctors to discuss the transplant details and road map on what will happen as soon as we check in. Boom's God mom also went into surgery today, thinking of her so much. I wish I could be there with her. But I'm glad her sister is there. May God be with her today and during her recovery.

November 22, 2019

Boom wanted to feel like a tourist this weekend, so we checked into a hotel in the city. Again, I felt so lucky to know people that are so giving. My former boss gave me a complimentary room to enjoy in the city. We toured the city; it was close to the holidays, so the NYC streets were already decorated. We had dinner in Times Square and bought great paintings from a vendor on the street. It was such a beautiful cold night; we went back to the room, and Boom jumped on the bed. She used to do that when she was a little girl. Such joy I felt that moment, but I was scared at what was ahead of us.

November 24, 2019

We hosted an early Thanksgiving dinner with our family today since we will be in the hospital for the upcoming holidays—Thanksgiving and Christmas. We hope to be home by New Years Eve. We had a scrumptious dinner with our family and close friends. We invited the priest over too, so he can bless Boom on her next chapter of healing. Another beautiful rainbow we saw outside today; I believe it's another sign of God telling us it will all be alright. I have so much faith these days. Our house looks so pretty with our X-mas decorations. We decided to decorate earlier this month since we knew we would not be home for the holidays.

November 26, 2019

We checked in to the hospital today, we packed up our home in three suit cases. We brought everything we could think of that would help us as we moved into the hospital for at least a minimum of five weeks. We bought a mattress topper so the bed would be more comfortable. We brought our own pillows. I was sad about leaving my home for a bit but I knew that when we returned, our Boom would be on the road to recovery. The new year is approaching, and we are hopeful that better things are coming. We decorated our room, and she did a simulation on radiation therapy.

November 29, 2019

Clowns came to our hospital bed to cheer Boom up. They make you laugh for a little bit but we are still in this small room with no roommates, of course, because of the transplant-related precaution reasons. I am glad we brought comfortable socks instead of those hospital socks. She feels cold, then hot. We have some hats for her "egg." We did our best to decorate our room with holiday decorations and a poster of her favorite rapper—Juice Wrld.

November 30, 2019

Boom gets a bicycle to stay active in her room. The nurses encouraged Boom to be active and move around in the room. Hospital staff has to come into room with protective gear, mask, gloves, and robe. I think we are all having a hard time being in this isolated room.

December 2, 2019

Boom had her first round of radiation. It's the era of pretty neat technology. I can see her through the monitors since I can't be in the room with her. I can talk to her and hear her through a mic. They can play your favorite music while you are in there so she requested to play Juice Wrld. That radiation was the longest seven minutes of my life. Actually, a total of fourteen minutes. She gets radiation on each side. My heart feels heavy, and I don't know really how I feel—scared, furious, etc. More so, I was happy that these are the final stages of her treatment. What I've seen today, I don't wish on even my worst enemy. So many times, I wished that I was going through this crisis than her going through it. Make her healthy again soon. Boom got recruited to be on the Today's show and had a special visit from a musician, Ingrid Michaelson. She was excited since she loves music.

December 3, 2019

Boom had more radiation today. The room is freezing cold. I hate being here with her. She wears a jacket, similar to a straightjacket, on her chest. As I look at the monitors and see her face, I see that somehow, she still manages to have a smile on her face. I wish I knew what she's thinking while this is happening to her. The radiation sound is a disturbing one; it irritates me. I'm overwhelmed with emotions.

December 4, 2019

Another round of radiation, one more day of this! All I can think is that tomorrow is the last day of this dreadful treatment; her body going through such an ordeal. God why can't I be in her place? But I know why. I'm not strong enough—I wouldn't make it through. You picked Boom because you know she can beat this.

December 5, 2019

It was the last session of radiation! She asked to listen to the song called "*It's the final countdown!*" Yes it is. She made it through twelve sessions. For four days straight, three times a day. God, I thought this would never end. What a champ my child is, and now tomorrow—transplant day! They say it's your new birthday. She feels defeated. Her arms are burnt and she feels exhausted. These days she has no appetite at all. Hospital food is not appetizing. I'm starting to get bored myself. Nights are tough; we constantly get awoken by nurses monitoring Boom's vital signs. She also needs help to get to the bathroom. She wants to go home.

December 6, 2019

I went to work this morning because her transplant was scheduled for the afternoon and got back to the hospital just in time. I don't know how much longer I can balance between work and living in the hospital. I feel overwhelmed. The transplant took about five minutes; they infused the donor's cells, and now we just wait for her counts to go up. As Boom said, "It smelled like a Cow's eyeball," as she dissected one with her class a year prior.

December 8, 2019

We did an x-ray today of her left chest. That side has collapsed, so she has early signs of pneumonia. I try my very best to get her out of bed and encourage her to shower, and I lotion her skin. She doesn't complain. She pops up with the little energy left in her. She's extremely sad today, since Juice Wrld passed away today.

December 10, 2019

Boom got a massage today; she's starting to get the after effects of the radiation. She looks pale, my poor kid. I continue to put lotion on her arms that are burnt. I tell her it will fade away with time. She's also developing a rash around her eyes. Doc gave us a special cream to put on her face. I feel like the walls of our room are closing in and we've only been here for a little over 2 weeks. We've had a few instances where the emergency alarm goes off on the floor for a patient and you can hear the medical team's footsteps running to the appropriate room. God please help them!

December 11, 2019

Boom had more x-rays done as they want to monitor her left lung. She keeps on hacking non-stop. They gave her something to calm her down. We have no visitors during the time we are here. Our families know that we will see them once we are back home. She had a mix of two drugs today, and she really got me scared. All the doctors were in here to monitor her. I feel helpless seeing her like this. Her feet are swollen, and she says she feels something sharp picking at her feet. Doctors say it's normal and gave us another cream just for her feet.

December 13, 2019

Her mucositis has worsened. They did a cat scan on her to see her esophagus. The test results are not good. She has bubbles in that area and those bubbles can rupture make her bleed internally. We got transferred to ICU for observation. Boom tells me she's only fighting for me; she wants to give up. My heart is broken.

December 14, 2019

Uncle Pete wrote a song called "*A Mother's Tears.*" It's so beautiful. I played it for Elle and she made a suggestion to play the annoying beep of the hospital machine in the background. I really hope my brother is discovered. He's a really talented being. I worry about him too; he has some health conditions, and I often wonder if he will make it.

December 16, 2019

They did an echo today of Boom's heart. Her pressure has been low, so they want to monitor her. Doctors say it's all the meds she is on. She's been on oxycodone for some time to manage her mucositis. She still can't swallow without pain. She's not eating and can't even sip on water.

December 17, 2019

I'm restless. More x-rays were carried out the past few days to monitor her pneumonia. It's way worse to sleep here in the ICU. Some days are longer than others. We've had some complications. She feels miserable. She has bad mucositis that doesn't allow her to swallow anything. All meds are IV. She's on heavy oxycodone. She doesn't look like herself at all. But we remain hopeful. Santa came to visit and we took a picture with the Grinch. We also had carolers outside our room singing Christmas songs. There's constant changing of medication, so we can put her at ease. All these meds fix one thing but mess other things. She's in pain and cries that she wants to go home. There's a church right across the street from the hospital and every time my hubby relieves me for a bit, I go there and pray. I pray that she gets healed and we get to go home soon.

December 23, 2019

Boom made her debut on the Today's show. The team here says she's a star. I know she is, and she will do great things. I know she was given this battle to overcome and help kids in the future fight this. We've met great nurses and doctors throughout our stay so far. Of course, we like some more than others! But all of them are here to make Boom better. Some have even shared their own personal stories that they've fought cancer and that inspired them to heal others. It is so inspirational, and I'm so glad I've met these individuals. Boom continues to feel sick; she has an upset stomach that keeps her in the bathroom just too many times. It's so uncomfortable for her; I so want to take her pain away.

December 24, 2019

It's Christmas Eve. Normally, we would be home hosting the holidays and gathering to open gifts. Instead we are here waiting. Her counts are trending up, not too quick but slow and steady. It seems like transplant was a success. I prayed for the donor. Boom hopes to meet the donor at some point in her life. They say it's possible but only if the donor agrees, you can only reach out in writing first after a year. I plan to also be a donor and help someone in need. The physical therapist was nice enough to get the doc's approval to go out of the room and have Boom take a walk to see the Christmas decorations on the ground floor of the hospital. It's been a month almost, and she wants to go out and get some fresh air. She loves the cold weather. I informed my employer that I will be resigning, working out departure dates. I look forward to just focusing on Boom's recovery. She did have another massage today.

December 25, 2019

It's X-mas Day—Santa came by and dropped off x-mas gifts. The hospital does a good job in uplifting your holiday spirits. So many families like us are spending time here, being a true support for their loved ones. I know we will all get through this; others may just take more time. But again, count my blessings every day. She's getting a little stronger day by day. We are finally out of ICU and back to a normal room. The ICU is more stressful and the rooms are much more uncomfortable. We hope to be home by next week. Doctors are very positive we will be home by New Years. We just want our beds and want her to open all of her presents underneath our X-mas tree. There are so many gifts from her classmates, teachers, and our family members. It gives her so much to look forward to.

December 26, 2019

They did an ultra sound today to check on her stomach area to see if there's anything concerning. But everything looks as normal as it can for a transplant patient. Days seem longer than others. She still hasn't had any solids to eat. I was showering her today and she said she didn't feel good as she was sitting on the bench. As soon as she told me that she was about to pass out, I immediately pulled the shower emergency cord. The whole medical team was in our room in a split second. It was overwhelming, they lifted her up to the bed and started placing all these gadgets on her to find out what was going on. I was losing my mind because all I can see is my baby girl crying for help and being scared. I just couldn't do anything, held her hand and prayed. She's okay now and resting but I'm not okay. Her body is weak and the water temperature of the shower made her react negatively.

December 27, 2019

Boom had a session of music therapy today. Music somehow lifts her spirits. She still feels this numbness on the tip of her fingers. That feeling started during chemo, and she still has it. Her hands also shake when she holds certain things. Doctors say it's normal and that she can take a particular medicine, but of course, she won't take it since it's not necessary. She hates adding another prescription to her routine.

December 29, 2019

She's starting to crave things again; she ate noodle soup almost after a month of not eating solid foods. I feel so happy to see her coming around. Doctors tell us we should be home later this week. They are very conservative as they don't like to discharge post-transplant patients before 45 days. Boom was very vocal that she wanted to go home, and she was emotional about everything. I myself reiterated that we needed to be home for our mental state. I believe once we are home, she will get stronger. She will be able to move around in the comfort of her home. She will open presents. There's so much to look forward to. We had a different treatment today called thiotepa which required to take a shower right after.

December 30, 2019

Boom had a long night again, so many interruptions. Can't get a good night's sleep. We hope to be home by tomorrow in our own beds. I washed loads of clothes and blankets to take home clean so I don't have to do laundry at home. We are so glad we purchased a mattress topper for Boom because the bed is super uncomfortable. Hubby took a lot home from our room today, so we don't have to pack up too much tomorrow. I'm so jealous he gets to go home often to our bed. But soon, we will all be there together.

December 31, 2019

Discharge day! After five weeks of being here, we are finally going home. The discharge team is preparing all of our medications and home instructions. She also got a massage before we left, and she was able to open all of her x-mas gifts under the tree. She was so happy! Just being home made her feel all better. I cooked, and we all sat down to finally have a home cooked dinner—just the three of us. We watched the Times Square special on TV and stayed until midnight to watch the ball drop, made a toast, and then curled up on our beds and finally had a good night's sleep. Thank you, Jesus.

January 1, 2020

Happy New Year! Put away all the stuff we had; the house was a mess since we left all our luggage out. It feels great to be home. Boom woke up better. I knew mentally we had to keep our sanity and just come home; everything else would fall into place. Grandma Rosey came over; she cooked for us. We also burned "el año Viejo"; it's an Ecuadorian tradition where we burn a big doll and stuff it with our old/new clothes with a letter. It symbolizes leaving the old memories in the past and bringing new hope into the new year. It felt good—it's not malice or voodoo. It just means 'out with the old and in with the new' considering what all of us have gone through. I hope we got rid of the negative energy. We cleansed the bad and let it bring us health in the upcoming year. I want Boom to heal quickly, so she can start to feel better emotionally and physically. Tomorrow is a follow up at the hospital. We had a quiet evening, and will get some rest now.

January 2, 2020

We had a good follow up today. It was a quick visit and we came home. I haven't seen my Pal since he has a cold and lives downstairs. He can't come up and visit because we need to protect our Boom. For the next 100 days, we have to be very mindful of visitors. Our routine will be hospital to home. She wears mask and gloves whenever she leaves the house. We are fanatic with Lysol wipes and spraying down everything. Grandma Rosey is not coming over too often either to protect Boom. She still has a poor appetite; she says it's her taste buds. Food doesn't taste the same anymore. Doctors say it's normal after transplant. School will be back in session soon so we've sorted out a plan with the school to learn and submit assignments remotely since she can't attend school until we see a sign of t-cells coming in.

January 4, 2020

We have a follow up today, the team wants to see us often about three days a week to make sure Boom is recovering well. We are very careful when we leave the house. She continually wears her mask and gloves. We keep our distance from people as we walk through the hallway and when we get on the elevator. If there are too many people, we wait for the next one.

January 6, 2020

We had a follow up today. Boom needed a boost of magnesium. When she gets these rounds of magnesium boosts, she feels hot inside and ill. She tends to take off her layers of clothes because she's so hot. She takes nine pills of magnesium a day because of this specific medicine she's on—to prevent graft versus host disease (GVHD). GVHD is very common after transplant. It may appear as a skin rash or internal concerns. She hasn't had any signs of this; therefore, so far, her body has accepted the donor's cells.

January 10, 2020

Boom had a follow up today, she needed another round of magnesium. These boosts continue making her ill, but she needs it for her body to recuperate. All of her count levels are trending up so we are happy.

January 13, 2020

Pal feels much better; he can finally visit Boom. Since his birthday was last week, we decided to celebrate it today along with Uncle Pete, as his birthday is next week. Boom finally had some guests, but with protective gear, of course. We had a nice dinner at home, and we baked some cupcakes. She still loves cupcakes 😊

January 14, 2020

We had another follow up visit today at the hospital. We now meet with the nutritionist since they are very focused on her gaining weight. So, we started on Ensure nutrition smoothies to increase her calorie intake. She is not a fan of them but she makes an effort. Her eating habits have changed for sure. Foods she enjoyed in the past are no longer in our shopping list. So ironic that about a year ago, I would tell Boom to not eat certain junk items and that it was too fattening. And now, I have to tell her to go ahead and eat all as she needed the calories.

January 17, 2020

She's taking her multi-vitamins and extra magnesium daily since she's on these post-transplant medications that decrease her magnesium. Boom is going to the bathroom a lot. Doctors would like to do an endoscopy if it gets worse just to see if everything is okay. I really don't want her to suffer more; she's been through enough. We will wait and see if it gets worse. Today was also my last day at work. I returned my company belongings and feel free. So now, I can just focus on her, since that alone is a full-time job.

January 20, 2020

Boom got her eyelashes done again; she now realizes that this is the last time she does them. She said she just wanted to use a good mascara. I'm all for it! It saves me money. She now wants to get into henna, fake freckles on her face... oh boy!

January 21, 2020

We had a follow up today, it was a long day. They started treating her for a virus that she has. The treatment is every other week. It's not contagious and normal after transplant. We got in early this morning and left at 8:00 p.m. and she wanted to pick up her new wig in Queens. So, of course I took her. The wig is gorgeous. We found a lady that makes wigs, and she was able to customize it just for Boom. She's happy; she's asleep now. I'm done for the day too.

January 24, 2020

The follow up went well, just another boost of magesium. She's craving McDonalds, against doc's orders to stay away from restaurants. But I went to pick her up a smoothie and chicken McNuggets—am I not supposed to fatten her up? These are the things Boom craves. Today is Day 49, so we are half way there!

January 27, 2020

We decided on a high school! We went to meet with the principal since we needed to make him aware of her condition in the upcoming year. She's very excited to be starting high school. May God bless her on this journey at the new school. The school is too big, and I'm concerned that she will have a tough time since she only knows her small elementary school. But I know Boom will be fine.

January 28, 2020

We got special permission to attend the National Honor Society induction ceremony at school. I'm very proud that she's been kicking cancer's ass, but she also has been focused on her school work. Doing schoolwork at home as she recovers has been a distraction. But she has her moments and tells me she wishes to be in school so she can be a kid again. I told her she will be with her silly classmates soon, and this will be behind her. She says she's missing on a lot of eighth grade activities. I keep saying, "It's going to be fine. Please let it be."

January 29, 2020

We had a follow up at hospital, she had another treatment where she had to breathe in, sort of like a nebulizer. It made her feel so ill. All these treatments every other week beat her up. T-cells, please come in. We took the test and hope that they are in. They do this test at the end of every month.

January 30, 2020

It's Grandma Rosey's 75th birthday. We went out to our favorite Mexican restaurant. It was quiet since everyone was at work and school. We had the whole restaurant to us, which meant lesser germs, of course. We had a nice lunch and celebrated her birthday. 🖤

January 31, 2020

We had a follow up again, no t-cells yet unfortunately. However, they also did a donor cell test, which indicated her body accepted the donor's cells 100%! Thank God! Boom had a hard time with this; she was hoping to have some t-cells so she could go back to school. She was so upset. There was nothing we could do. There's nothing we can take or eat to speed up the process. It's just the waiting game all over again just like we were waiting on counts at the hospital.

February 2, 2020

We had our families over, and we were again grateful for our cheerleaders. We had some good food and hung out for a bit. These visits are shorter than in the past, as everyone knows that she needs her rest and that we still need to minimize any risk of Boom getting sick. I've been noticing that she forgets things or doesn't remember—it's the famous saying of "chemo brain." I guess, in some way, it is better that she doesn't remember some things.

February 4, 2020

We had a follow up today, she did a bit of tai-chi at the hospital as we waited to begin treatment. She puked again and doesn't feel well. These treatments take her about two whole days to recuperate. Depending on what time her initial treatment began, I will need to give her medicines eight hours after that, so I had to wake her up at 2:00 a.m. to give her the last dose of medicines. I feel so bad for waking her up as she's sound asleep and tired from today.

February 9, 2020

We went to the park today since it was a beautiful weather. Doctors said it was fine going out now and getting fresh air. Of course, that doesn't mean we are going to crowded malls or concerts. But we can definitely start going out and getting air. I took great pictures of her; I'm like her paparazzi these days—trying to capture every moment of recovery. It's so nice indeed… Day 65.

February 14, 2020

I dropped her off at school today for Valentine's Day. Doctors said it was okay since it was just for a little while. I bought cute masks for the students in her class. It was so sweet of her teacher to send me a group picture. She was so happy visiting them. She will always be my Valentine.

February 16, 2020

We went to the park again. She got on the swing. She loves the swings. I took some nice photos again of her. She's so beautiful and breathtaking. I wish she could see it.

February 18, 2020

We had a follow up today along with physical therapy at the hospital. They work on her leg a lot so she can get strength back in her left leg. Her back bothers her more in the evening after physical therapy. My hubby gives her back massages, since she says I don't know how to. LOL. We also give her scalp massages to stimulate her hair growth. She loves using her special oils. Boom is having a tough time sleeping at nights. She does not fall asleep now until after midnight. We have tried Melatonin but again she's not a fan of taking extra stuff that is not necessary. They say cancer patients develop PTSD-Posttraumatic stress disorder- because of their traumatic experience. We will need to monitor this as she is now getting flashbacks on things that occurred at the hospital. Even a whiff of a certain food or drink takes her back to crazy moments and makes her nauseous. In addition, noises that are similar to the beeping of the IV pump machine—like an amber alert that goes off on the phone— freak her out. My heart breaks.

February 21, 2020

We are staying at the Hamptons this week for her birthday tonight and tomorrow. We had such a great day today; we reserved an igloo and had some appetizers and drinks. We also had dinner reservations by the water tonight. So thankful I can celebrate another year. At times, I felt we wouldn't get here. On Sunday, we will be having just the family and her teacher over to celebrate her birthday. As a present, we special ordered her a name plate with her name, but the letter "L" are cancer ribbons. My former coworker was kind enough to design it for me, and I had my jeweler make it.

February 23, 2020

We had our families over today. Had a nice quiet lunch and spent some time together. It was a beautiful weather day with windows open and fresh air flowing. I had everyone wear a mask and surgical gown. To think, fourteen years ago, I literally gave birth to my hero. I definitely didn't want this battling journey for her, but I know she was built to overcome this and embrace whatever life has to offer her. As they say, God doesn't give you anything you can't handle and He was right just giving us one child. She received nice gifts, especially rainbow roses from her Godmother.

February 24, 2020

I took her to school today to celebrate her birthday with the class. I ordered pizza and brought in treats for her class. I'm glad she was able to celebrate her last year at this school. High school is a different world. The kids wore masks, and I had reminded the teacher to tell them not to embrace Boom, just air high-five!

February 25, 2020

We had a follow up today, we are finally seeing her gain a few pounds. Not like where we want it to be, but not necessary for an endoscopy. It's nice that we are down to one day weekly visit these days.

February 26, 2020

It's Ash Wednesday. We went to evening mass to receive our ashes. This is a time for sacrifice and not eating meat on Wednesdays. I also look forward to our fanesca soon—it's our Good Friday festive soup that Grandma Rosey makes. I look forward to this season, where spring is just right around the corner.

February 28, 2020

We had a follow up today, she had treatment today along with physical therapy. Her leg is starting to feel better but they ordered a brace for her to use when she's laying on her bed and doing homework.

February 29, 2020

We received some gifts from my beautiful breast cancer survivor cousin in Mexico. She sent Boom tools to paint. They're called mandala, we are going to experiment this and see what it is all about. Boom loves painting so we will try it out. Of course, I'll paint with a wine glass. We had a follow up today at the hospital where we took the famous t-cell test. Let's see how she does.

March 3, 2020

We have three t-cells in! Not a whole lot to report but it's something! Boom was really upset again; she was hoping to have more. But I made her see that at least it's in. We went for a ride so she can take her mind off things.

March 6, 2020

We went to her school mass; she was altering for this mass. I'm so happy she will be back to serving masses as an alter girl. Boom says she misses that. The 100th day is approaching soon, we are relieved. I trust the worst is almost behind us.

March 8, 2020

We went to the park today. It was another beautiful weather day. We are back to taking family selfies. There is a lot of media coverage on TV about Corona Virus affecting the US. It's pretty concerning, considering we are taking extra care of Boom and ourselves these days.

March 9, 2020

She ordered personalized Vans sneakers with cancer ribbons. She now wants to share with the world she beat this and help other children going through the same. I fully support her to share her story and not be ashamed. I've been private as well, but recently, I had posted on social media for Boom's birthday about our journey.

March 10, 2020

This whole Covis-19 pandemic is a bit scary; people are starting to die from this virus. Every day, every second, there are more cases. It's affecting everyone—not only the immune compromised population but also the healthy people. It's a bit nerve-racking but again, I pray this doesn't affect us. I think God knows we've been battling our own crisis, and I trust that's what we needed to go through.

March 13, 2020

The principal has announced Boom's school closure because of the pandemic. I feel like the world is post-transplant with us now! Boom, and now all kids, will be doing school remotely. Just when we were getting back a bit of normalcy into our lives, this crap hits us. God help us all.

March 14, 2020

We went to the park again, but we took some sandwiches and refreshments and ate in the trunk of our car. It was another beautiful day. I drove back home, while Boom and hubby sat in the trunk with the back jeep window open. She said we must do this again, she had fun. We took some more fun pictures!

March 15, 2020

I saw more bad news in the media about the Covis-19 pandemic. Not only are there school closures but businesses are starting to close too. Wow… Jobs are being eliminated; businesses are starting to close. It's tough to be a Human Resources professional right now, telling a whole lot of people that they're jobless. The laws are changing to accommodate this crisis. It's going to be a tough market to get back into. Perhaps employers will now see that remote work is an option and that you can still be successful at your job. Today marks Boom's 100th day after transplant! She made it.

March 17, 2020

Happy St. Patrick's Day! The bars and restaurants are all closed officially. But that won't take us away from celebrating. I had Boom dress up in her green gear, and I cooked corn beef and cabbage. Everyone is at home trying to avoid the Corona virus.

March 18, 2020

Things drastically changed; we don't have physical contact with our usual doctors. They are reducing any form of contact. However, we had to do our weekly blood work, so we did that and the doc called us over the phone while at the hospital. We had another treatment scheduled, so we took care of it today.

March 24, 2020

This Corona Virus is sure a mess. We have more cases than China right now. I'm a little frantic of hubby still going to work and bringing something back home and getting us sick. I've told Mom just to come once a week. I'm also worried about her living alone. Glad my Pal is stuck in Ecuador, one less parent to think about here. We had our usual bi-weekly virus treatment today; Boom was so sick. We had to pause for some time until she got better. She had an allergic reaction, and said her face and tongue were numb. We got out so late from there tonight. I'm beat and so is she.

March 31, 2020

We had the t-cell test today. We trust we have more t-cells lined up. Boom's hair has grown in significantly. Spoke with Pal in Ecuador, and he says things are pretty horrible there, and that people are dying on the streets with this terrible virus. Hubby started his compressed work schedule today; he will be working three days only in the office and other days remotely. I'm still concerned since some of his co-workers have been testing positive for this virus. God please protect our daughter.

April 1, 2020

Waiting on results still… did some grocery online shopping as it's too scary to even go out. I've told my mom not to go out. They just sent a letter that school remote learning will be extended until April 30th. Initially, it was April 20th. Palm Sunday and Easter mass will be televised since church is closed. It's incredible to see TV shows being hosted in homes and not in studios anymore. We have a new way of life. Media says the peak of deaths will be this month and will get better by June. There are no sports to watch. US Open Tennis stadium that Boom and I are so used to going for games are being converted to a medical center with beds. We may not even have a US Open this year and if does happen there will be no fans- how sad.

April 2, 2020

Woo hoo! Elle's t-cells are at 189! We are super excited and grateful. Since her t-cells have increased, she doesn't have the virus anymore; therefore, she doesn't need to do those treatments that made her ill. We also don't have to go weekly anymore for visits. We will see them in two weeks, even better with this pandemic taken over the world. We want to minimize any exposure in the hospital.

April 5, 2020

We watched Palm Sunday mass on TV today. It's crazy how we can't go to mass and receive our palms. People are staying safe in their homes. It's tough as we are having spring-like weather. I try not to watch the news; it just gives me more anxiety. Mom is in her home. She's having difficulty too since she likes to go out. We are all getting cabin fever. The hubby is now just going to work two days and working from home three days. We are all going to drive each other insane. I'm starting to look for work as unemployment won't cover all my monthly bills. And my culinary, bartending, and cleaning skills are getting dated!

April 6, 2020

The Covid pandemic has kept us isolated even more. I placed my online grocery shopping for the week; even they are backed up. My pick-up date was pushed by a day. No big deal if we don't drink milk or eat rice for a day. These days you eat what's in your fridge. I'm a little hesitant in picking up food since I don't know who's infected. God bless those essential workers that have to go to work and are in the front line of this disaster, putting their lives and families at stake. We received a box of treats today from our close friend in Delaware. He sent Easter gifts to Boom and a lot of religious gifts that he bought in Columbia. He's so thoughtful and sweet throughout this. It brightened Boom's day. We made some great Columbian coffee too!

April 7, 2020

I received my grocery order and I wiped down all items with Lysol wipes. It's so different how we are so paranoid. Well, we've been paranoid since after transplant, but now it's on a different level. Grandma Rosey came over and we had our traditional soup for Good Friday. Today was a quiet day. It was a day of religious reflection.

April 8, 2020

I had a talk with another parent today going through a similar journey. I always like to talk to parents these days and share with them my story. I always tell the hospital to share my contact information with parents or a teenager if they want to talk to Boom. We would be glad to help. For some reason, it gives me some comfort just telling a parent it's going to be okay and that I was in their shoes and it may feel that it's not going to get better but it certainly will. One has to keep the faith and be strong.

April 12, 2020

It is Easter Sunday today, and we did an egg hunt for Boom in the yard. We watched Easter mass on TV. We usually have family over on this day. But now everyone is in their respective homes. A whole new way of life. Non-essential workers are working from home and those who are essential, need to be at work. It will take time for the economy to bounce back. Until then, we take this extra time to do a lot of soul searching; along with my job search. An added weekly unemployment allowance is being granted for everyone unemployed to help during these economic crises. You are allowed to call banks and postpone your mortgage, student loans etc… not sure I'm going to do that since you still have to pay at some point.

April 14, 2020

We had a quick hospital visit today. They checked her blood count, and we hardly have any physical contact with the doctors anymore because of the Covid nightmare. Good thing is that, since transplant, as soon as we get to the hospital, they put us in an isolated back patient room so Boom is not exposed to infections. So far so good. This pandemic has actually given her more time to heal and I know I'm just looking at *the silver lining. Timing was surely everything. It has allowed her body to heal more* especially since the school year apparently will be remote until June. Boom will start her freshmen year in high school in the Fall—healthy! God willing schools be back to normal by then.

April 16, 2020

We try to keep busy during these quarantine days. Boom has been on Easter recess from school, so she's getting a break. However, she still has some assignments to complete. We put on our fire pit today in the yard and roasted some marshmallows. It was a nice chilly evening and we were all bundled up. These are the moments that I think back on; all I have missed out on with my busy career life. But I'm glad I have the opportunity to make up for lost time. God has certainly given me a second chance. I pray for all the Covid patients and their families. There are so many families that can't get a proper burial because its mayhem. I've had some close friends that have lost their family members because of Covid and they were cancer patients. It makes me nervous, but I trust we already went through our battle.

April 21, 2020

We had our follow up genetic testing call today with the team. Boom took a genetic test back in November and we finally received the results today. It was an interesting call, to say the least. The testing confirmed that Boom doesn't have a genetic disposition that caused her cancer. In addition, she doesn't carry a gene that she can pass off to her children. Boom is happy to hear this. They did confirm that she does carry an SDS-Shwachman Diamond syndrome- gene that may cause her kids to have some health complications. Although, they say it's very common in people, it's recommended that once she starts family planning, she has her partner tested so they can confirm whether he has it or not. On the other hand, they recommended for hubby and I to get tested for aplastic anemia, so we will be getting a blood test next month at our follow up. Overall, we were pleased with the call. However, as a parent you always wonder, 'How my kid got this, was it something I did wrong—was it nutrition? Is it something environmental; where we live or a place we visited?' It's just something I'll never have closure to.

April 24, 2020

I was just talking about families going through challenges with Coronavirus. We just lost my hubby's grandmother due to this. It was so sad. We had to say our farewells via FaceTime. My hubby and his family are dealing with the aftermath in preparation of her burial. Elle lost her great-grand mom. We are blessed to have spent time with her. There are so many deaths occurring during this pandemic. Some of my friends are also losing their loved ones. New York will be the last to re-open, but we remain hopeful. My mom-in-law tested positive as well and is fighting it daily. She has her good days and not-so-good days. We pray she feels better soon and that she finds some comfort in losing her mom too.

April 30, 2020

Boom took her monthly t-test today. We had our standard follow up with blood counts. She gained two pounds, which we are very happy about! Now, we wait for results next week. Our last t-test count was 189. Now we hope to be over 300. Praying…

May 1, 2020

Wow! Another month upon us. How quick time is flying by. Next month will be a year that my Boom started her journey. I hosted a Zoom happy hour call today with my Human Resources friends. I love to network and since we can't dine or wine out, I decided to sip some wine virtually with them. It was a good call. We all connected and everyone was able to share their stories on how Coronavirus has affected them both professionally and personally. A few of us are unemployed and seeking employment; however, others are still employed and working remotely. The Arch Diocese announced again today that schools will remain closed for the rest of the school year. Boom will continue her remote learning; she's really bummed about it since she anxiously wanted to get back. So now she will have no graduation or prom (just like many other students). I tell her that this extension of her recovery was a blessing in disguise; she will be able to focus on herself and be ready for high school. I hope she gets it; it's hard for her to accept it.

May 3, 2020

Today was a beautiful Sunday. Gosh, the weather is getting gorgeous outside. It almost hit 80 degrees today. We grilled for dinner and did marshmallows on the fire pit this evening. We try to do lots of fun stuff while in quarantine. I ordered a snow cone machine and some pretzels and we had a Carnival day indoors. We need to be creative so we don't go out of our minds. I walk in circles in my yard just to get my three miles in and use the elliptical to move my muscles. I definitely don't want to gain more weight once this is over! Doing dishes, cooking, and doing laundry doesn't help much for exercise.

May 6, 2020

Today is Boom's 5th month birthday (post-transplant). So happy to see she's getting stronger and healthier. She's eating more these days, slowly gaining 2 lbs. per week. In the past, I always had to ask her, "What you want to eat, are you hungry? You should eat." Now, she helps herself to the fridge! That's success! Overall, it was a good day.

May 10, 2020

Happy Mother's Day! I feel blessed that I can share another year with Grandma Rosey and Boom. Honestly, didn't think I was going to be able to celebrate another year with Boom. It was tough to see your baby girl starting to deteriorate when she first started her journey. However, fast forward, she has remained defiant. We had a nice intimate Mother's Day. Grandma Rosey came over. She cooked and we had a nice early dinner. Boom got me cute gifts—a wine glass that I love so much! And a necklace to symbolize that I'm also a champ. She told me she couldn't have done it without me. These are the moments that I will always cherish.

May 12, 2020

Such a beautiful day outside today—we planted jalapenos, tomatoes, and basil. Hubby went to pick up soil to plant in the yard. This is the first time we gardened. Both of us don't have green thumbs but let's see if Boom does! We also grilled outside since the weather was gorgeous. I'm starting to have some interview video calls lined up so looking forward to that. The good news is that cases have gone down and there's less people checking into the hospitals. Some of the added resource places we had like Javits Center have closed since we don't need these medical locations anymore. Other states are opening their businesses slowly. We are starting to see some positive movement globally. However, don't think we will all be safe until a Corona vaccine is out there, which won't happen until perhaps early next year or maybe it will be available right after the elections?

May 13, 2020

Boom was craving Taco Bell so we drove to New Jersey since there are no open locations in Staten Island right now. The mall is still closed. It was a nice day anyway, so we did drive through and ate in the parking lot in the shade, our "car picnic." We also passed by a nice mural in Staten Island before we went home. I enjoy taking pictures of Boom. I know she will definitely reflect back on these moments. She's literally less than a month away from graduating middle school. Then I officially have myself a high schooler! Yikes. Uncle Phil who lives in North Carolina. He's a medical responder; however, he hurt his foot so he will be in a cast for six weeks, perhaps a blessing as well during this pandemic. He won't expose himself during this time.

May 14, 2020

I helped Mom today with her vehicle to get the oil changed and inspection done. She spent some time with us, and we did a campfire and roasted some marshmallows in the yard. Boom really misses her Grandma Rosey. Boom says, "I wish we can just go back to normal, where you are back at work and Grandma stays here." I tell her, "Soon we will once the job market gets better, I'll be able to land a job and Grandma Rosey can come back and stay with us." Boom says she has this feeling that this is not the end of her battle. She says she will be faced with another challenge in her life. I told her not to focus on it. Focus on what you've overcome and that you are healing. And if God sends us another cross to bear, then we will embrace and kick ass again. It makes me wonder if this gut feeling will come true. She also wants to see a medium, but I'm not ready for it.

May 15, 2020

Summer is near! Weather is gorgeous. Boom had her school Zoom call outside on the deck. She's kept busy with her homework and school assignments. She's doing a lot of videos for her assignments. I'm not sure if it's for a time capsule surprise for graduation. Her school is planning some fun grad events. We took a ride and went for some ice cream and stopped by the beach to take some pictures, of course! Boom even craved a burger—so I picked up Shake Shack. She loved it!

May 18, 2020

Today there was a drive through at Boom's school parking lot. The principal and teachers were there to hand out graduation treats. It was a nice event; everyone had their vehicles decorated. The cars lined up and paraded through the parking lot; honking their horns and making noise! Boom was excited as she found some comfort being back on school grounds. She's been doing this remote learning since late November, way before this pandemic started. We picked up her personal belongings from her classroom since she is not returning. High school, here we come!

May 20, 2020

Went on a physical interview, of course, practicing social distancing, and I believe it went very well. I found it so strange not to shake hands when you introduce yourself or sit in a conference room with people on the other side of the table. I have a few more video calls this week on other potential opportunities. It's a slow process since people tend to be out of the office during the summer. Memorial Day weekend is coming up in the next couple of days. We really can't travel anymore. We will open our pool this weekend as weather is supposed to be nice. Next week, we have our monthly follow up. I look forward to knowing Boom's t-test results again.

May 25, 2020

God Bless America. This day focuses on the many individuals who served and died for our country and freedom. It was another beautiful day; summer is surely really close. I hope this pandemic gets better for sure. We put on the grill today and barbecued. It's a bit sad not being able to have family over and it's just the three of us, but I know we have each other. This pandemic is not just about the virus but it's a time of depression as well. Not being able to leave your house and do your normal activity really can beat you down. I just don't lose hope.

May 26, 2020

We went for Boom's monthly follow up today. The counts look great. We will await t-cell count. One of Boom's amazing doctors told us that she will be leaving the hospital and relocating to another state. We are so happy for her; however, at the same time, we are really going to miss her. She was right by our side for the past year. We are back in the hospital next week since Boom has to get treated for something that is lower than usual. But overall, she's feeling good and is looking forward to being over 200 on her t-cells and holding her turtle again! Once we are over this amount, she can stop taking the current meds that she's on. I'm sure we are well over that number. We are about a month away from her one-year diagnosis anniversary and we are planning a special surprise for Boom. Although we see signs of her recovery, she still has her toe nails and finger nails falling off, which are the after effects of radiation.

May 27, 2020

Woohoo! We received some great news: Boom's t-cells are well over 200! 234 to be exact. We are stoked! We even scheduled a tennis lesson outdoors again. Our local tennis center is not open yet due to the pandemic. However, New Jersey tennis outside courts are open, we will meet her coach this weekend. I'm so proud of her; she's really kicked ass the past year. I feel blessed that she's come out of this stronger and a more compassionate young lady. She still gets headaches. On occasion, a migraine would occur and her back aches a lot, but again, it's part of the recovery.

May 29, 2020

Boom did my pedicure and manicure; I had a spa day! All salons are still closed, until then Boom will be my manicurist. She did a good job I must say! Boom is finishing up her school work in the next two weeks. She was telling me about the book she just read, "To Kill a Mockingbird." I remember reading it too back when I was in elementary school. Boom makes a good point that the discrimination back in the 1930s hasn't changed much. We continue to have hatred toward others that don't look like us. It's devastating, that people can be so evil and kill others because of their color of skin. Recently, there have been a lot of protests not only in NYC but in main cities about a recent case of a cop that was supposed to help take care of our civilians and our community, but did the exact opposite. It is such a shame to still be living in a world where there are still ignorant souls. May God help them find peace.

May 30, 2020

Boom was back on the tennis courts today; it was a hot day too! She looked so happy, being able to work on her rhythm again. What a sport!? She was beat at the end; she was staying hydrated of course. I was a bit nervous; I certainly don't want her to faint out there. But again, I trust she is going to be fine, and besides, her coach has given her breaks in between. We had a nice day at the park. We then grabbed some lunch and ate at home. Since it was a warm day, Boom went into the pool. What an amazing day to see her do things that she enjoys. I count my blessings every day.

May 31, 2020

Boom's teacher informed me today that Boom is the salutatorian of her class. I'm so proud of her, considering all her obstacles she made it to the top of her class. Her drive-in graduation is in about two weeks. I am looking forward to it. This chapter ends and a new chapter begins.

June 1, 2020

Uncle Pete went to take the Covid test today. He hasn't been feeling well this past week. I encouraged him to take it since Grandma Rosey drops off food to him so I don't want her to get sick. She comes here once a week, so I certainly don't want her spreading anything. We will await results; it takes usually two days or so. I continue to have calls for potential job opportunities; however, nothing has planned out yet. Employers are taking their time since Phase one of re-opening New York starts on Monday. There are four phases so we really won't see the final phase until perhaps end of next month or August. I know that when I go back to work, offices will be a different world. I have my work cut out for me as an HR professional. There's a demand for Diversity and Inclusion experts in the workplace. We will see what this summer will bring. Keep praying that the universe takes a positive direction.

June 3, 2020

Uncle Pete tested negative, which is great! He did both tests, the one that is done as a nose swab, and the antibodies test. I feel relieved since I was worrying about him and Grandma Rosey. We picked up Boom's cap and gown today at school. She has written her salutatorian speech and is practicing for next week. We also joined a Zoom call this evening from her future high school to discuss the options for classes in September. Obviously, we don't know how school life will be in the Fall; however, the school already is talking about plans of dividing the kids into groups so you don't have so many students at the same time in the building. A lot of remote learning will continue to occur if we don't gain back a bit of normalcy. At least we are having early conversations on what to expect if schools don't open back up. Cleaning is a priority of course; the school will have a new filter system with UV lights to cleanse the air. There are also thermal cameras that will be installed in the school to scan body temperatures. Wiping down everything with Lysol wipes has been my daily routine since we came home from the hospital back on December 31st after Boom's transplant. Now we just go to the extreme of cleaning our shoes when we come back from the outside, wiping down groceries from the supermarket. I'm sure all these cleaning products in a few years will be a health hazard for us. It's an absurd time and all we can do is take it, one day at a time.

June 6, 2020

Boom is six-months-old today—post transplant! It's been a long road and she's recovering slowly. Doctors say it takes a good year to get your body back after chemo, radiation and transplant. I can see the transformation in her physically and mentally. She's blossoming into a young beautiful lady but of course she doesn't see it. She doubts herself and lacks confidence but I know she will find her way. She will have these scars all of her life. I didn't want this for my child but I know there's a reason why. Besides our world turning, the outside world is still abrupt – New York City even has a curfew tonight. Only essential workers have a valid reason to be on the street.

June 12, 2020

Boom's graduation day! What a special day it was. Boom articulated her speech wonderfully and projected her voice very well. The school did a great job arranging the ceremony. Each vehicle had their own spot in the parking lot, and the families cheered on by their car. A small stage was set up so that the kids can receive their diploma and awards. It was a hot day to keep those masks, plus the graduation gowns and caps. We were fortunate to have a beautiful ceremony, considering other graduating students have a virtual or just a drive-by-your-home graduation. Kudos to our principal and teachers for planning a successful event. Boom went home with several awards for her hard work this year. I'm super proud of my baby.

June 13, 2020

We decided to take a drive to Delaware and visit a dear friend by the lake. Right now, they are allowing NY plates to travel. We've been quarantined for some time so we want to get some fresh ocean air. We had an enjoyable time this weekend. We even took a drive to Assateague and Ocean City, Maryland, by the shore to take some pics and feel our feet in the sand. It was a nice short break from the city. These times I wish we had a second home out of the city. New York is not to my liking anymore; you can tell from this pandemic that it's been a long process to open up because we are such an overpopulated city. I also believe it would be a great option to move into a better environment for Boom. I just wish I knew what could have prevented all this but I know I will never know. We just need to better control the present and future.

June 15, 2020

Grandma Rosey went to take the Covid test since we just wanted comfort of mind. We should know in a couple of days. Boom wants to be able to hug her grand mom! I'm still interviewing but employers are really not in a rush to hire until September. More layoffs are happening in the hospitality industry and unemployment rate continues to increase in some industries. It's tough all around, but again, we remain hopeful and optimistic that the economy will get better. I signed up Boom for two virtual summer camps starting next month. In addition, she will also be receiving a summer homework packet from her High School that will keep her busy. I have to also see when I order her new school uniform which I probably can't go into a physical store until the later part of next month during Phase 4 of New York City re-opening.

June 18, 2020

Grandma Rosey tested negative! Good news. I'll be taking mine next week when I go get my physical. I really haven't been anywhere but at home with Boom, so I should be fine. We went to a drive-in movie tonight, went to see Toy Story. Drive-in pop ups will be more popular these days since the movie theatres are not open yet, and they will probably not be the most ideal place to hang out. I spoke to the Make-A-Wish rep, and due to the pandemic, Boom's Make A Wish is being placed on hold. They will re-visit her wish later this year and see if they can grant it or continue to place it on hold until the world is in a better place. I'm starting to run out of pages in this journal. Time to get a new one soon.

June 21, 2020

We had a quiet Father's Day today. We did breakfast in bed for hubby and stayed in the pool almost the whole afternoon. We ordered hibachi and sushi for dinner. Pal is still in Ecuador. The airport just opened this month but he is going to stick around a little bit longer since his job has him on layoff until October. Covid cases are starting to spike up in other states like Florida and Texas. This crisis surely is not going away anytime soon. The hospitality business is suffering since there are not much tourists in NYC. A toast to all fathers who have made an impact on a child's life, this is truly important.

June 22, 2020

Boom had her monthly follow up today. No t-test done. Since she's over the 200 count, there's no need to do it every month. Blood counts look all good. Boom started her vaccines today. She got four of them. Next month, she will receive another series. We need to administer the same shots that she got as a baby because everything has been wiped out of her system since going through treatments and transplant. She was in a little pain for the rest of the day on her arms but nothing she couldn't handle… (my strong cookie)! It was a quick visit; we spoke to the doc and I went through my list of questions because every week I go into my notes section on my phone and ask away. Doctor says we are down to now every two months for follow up. So next month is just vaccines. The was no need to see doctors. In August, Boom will have her medi-port removed. Another clear sign of recovery.

June 26, 2020

A year ago, we started our journey! Today was a day focused on gratitude and her tremendous recovery. We took Boom to the beach and had doves fly out of a basket. It was a huge surprise for Boom. She actually thought we were surprising her with a dog. The lady that owns the doves met us at the beach. It's so interesting how these doves are trained to fly high into the sky but then fly back to her home. The three doves were a sign of the Father, the Son and the Holy Spirit. We took beautiful pictures on the beach. Again, this day was all about Boom. I find it hard to believe just a year ago we were at the hospital receiving the devastating news and here we are, blessed to have gone through this bumpy journey. We went out for ice cream and pizza—Boom's favorite. We also stayed in the pool for the rest of the afternoon. We prayed with Grandma Rosey and planned a lovely evening. We did a fire pit and burned Boom's meds since she's off of all medicines now. We also had lanterns fly away into the dark sky, so beautiful to watch it get lost but still see that light far, far away. This was very symbolic since I always saw light in the darkest moments. Boom made a couple of wishes as we let the lanterns go. I hope they all come true. Amen.

I end this journal here because it was a big year for my family and I. I encourage you if you are going through your own battle, to write your thoughts down. I believe when you reflect on them, you will be in a better place. We sure are. Don't lose faith and hope. For all the heroes and those that are standing by their side—you are so brave—don't give up. It is okay to talk about your mental health and it's okay to be vulnerable. Be persistent with doctors. If you feel something is wrong, follow your gut. Do not settle for 'it's just a phase!' At this very moment, the world is upside down; Covid-19 pandemic continues, and racism, violence, and the police brutality are not going away anytime soon. In addition, it's election year and the political game is at the forefront. Still, find a way to focus on the positivity and be grateful for what you have. And call out for help—you cannot do it alone. I know this is just the beginning of my daughter's journey. She will pave the way and achieve so much. She is already gotten a head start at fourteen. She is ready to fight any obstacle! **Boom!**

BOOK ACKNOWLEDGEMENTS:

I must start off by thanking my daughter, my hero, who is an inspiration. You truly fill my heart with pride and meaning. And to my hubby: with our love, we created a beautiful human being. And to all the special people in our lives who share this blessed journey of life with us.

ABOUT THE AUTHOR:

Ellen was born and raised in Queens, NY. Sister to an older and younger brother, Peter and Philip. She is the daughter of hard-working parents who were immigrants from Ecuador, Rosa and Pedro. She's a wife to her high school sweetheart, Tony. Ellen has a double Master's Degree in Human Resources. She enjoys working with people and finds labor law fascinating. In her free time, she enjoys spending time with Elle, her ONEderful daughter and her hubby. She loves to travel, is a foodie, and enjoys margaritas on the beach. She's grateful in sharing her story, and hopes it inspires caretakers to write about their own life experiences. She quotes, "Writing and sharing my thoughts has helped my mental health and I hope it helps others to hold on to faith in the darkest moments."

POSTLUDE OF A GRATEFUL
SURVIVOR DUDE(TTE) ♥

Elle Barrera aka **BOOM**! ✵

June 26th and the year alone (2019) was a big miss. You heard it from Mom first.. aka the best mother I can possibly ask for. If I had to tell you anything about my momma!!.. She is sweet, caring and carries her bulky journal everywhere you can imagine! She's written down about my meds, chemos, doctors who thought she was my sister.., and things that I couldn't remember until I read it again ...but never her own accomplishments. She's taught me to take life as it comes.. never ever leaving my side. *No matter how rough or tough! You are one in a zillion.*

She has made me to the person I am today.. I am who I am because of her..

I am so proud of you Momma, 'te quiero hasta la luna ida y vuelta' ♥ Now let's talk

about the strongest person reading this **YOU**.. whether you are a survivor of life's curve balls, cancer champ, doctor, nurse, mother, father, daughter, son or just someone who needs a helping hand, struggling with depression or PTSD ..someone who battles their own demons.., <u>YOU ARE SO LOVED</u>. If I can turn back time to tell myself that everything was going to be okay.. I would. I am unfortunately not a time traveler.. So I'm here to tell you….

YOU CAN MAKE IT THROUGH.

"Life is a <u>marathon</u>, not a <u>sprint</u>" September of 2019.... I was so obsessed with showing no evidence of disease and trying to do everything to ensure that. It made me feel like I failed somehow by still having cancer. I know now that I can truly live with the aftermath of cancer and appreciate each day I'm alive and feeling well, and still have hope for the future.

Think the impossible.. & make it possible! All of me believes, early dedication saved my life.., know it is NEVER too late. As I said in my graduation speech (June 12th), "A piece of advice that I can share is live a life of love & meaning.. make the world a better and **kinder** place no matter what **race** we are.. & work to reshape the future.. And if you fall or get pushed down again… *get back up..* AND **DO IT AGAIN**."

I will continue to battle to the very end & I hope you do too! I am thankful for being alive. I am thankful for keeping positivity near me, always at reach and never far out. Most of all, I am thankful for my mom sharing my story with you!!

For cancer champions.. Keep a blanket by you to keep you warm & vibe to your favorite songs :)

DON'T FORGET YOU ARE BEAUTIFUL and have wonderful outer & inner beauty and I have the CT of your scan to prove it!!

bald is beautiful.

And to all.. "Be positive about the future, Then the road ahead will be worth it."

-Denise Austin

Thank you to my medical team.. You know who you are!

…hmmmm.. maybe someday I'll publish my very own journal too.

For sneak peeks follow me on instagram! @sneakii.ii.. my dms are always always always open to chat!

Credits for book cover: www.thungdesign.com